INDIAN HEARTS

VOICE OF THE SOUL

RANJAN YADAV

Copyright © Ranjan Yadav
All Rights Reserved.

This book has been self-published with all reasonable efforts taken to make the material error-free by the author. No part of this book shall be used, reproduced in any manner whatsoever without written permission from the author, except in the case of brief quotations embodied in critical articles and reviews.

The Author of this book is solely responsible and liable for its content including but not limited to the views, representations, descriptions, statements, information, opinions and references ["Content"]. The Content of this book shall not constitute or be construed or deemed to reflect the opinion or expression of the Publisher or Editor. Neither the Publisher nor Editor endorse or approve the Content of this book or guarantee the reliability, accuracy or completeness of the Content published herein and do not make any representations or warranties of any kind, express or implied, including but not limited to the implied warranties of merchantability, fitness for a particular purpose. The Publisher and Editor shall not be liable whatsoever for any errors, omissions, whether such errors or omissions result from negligence, accident, or any other cause or claims for loss or damages of any kind, including without limitation, indirect or consequential loss or damage arising out of use, inability to use, or about the reliability, accuracy or sufficiency of the information contained in this book.

Made with ♥ on the Notion Press Platform
www.notionpress.com

To My Mother...

My mother doesn't know to write any alphabet. She has never got a chance to go to school, yet she is wise, she knows the improtance of education. When I was a small child, She bought a slate and pencil to write in, and gave me. She sent me shool, so that I might get good education.When I grew up a bit more, she put her hand on my head, and told, "My son, you have to go far in the world of education because few poeple are educated in this village." She provided me everything that I needed in school, college and university.I obeyed my mother, laboured hard and completed my Post Graduate.I started to write English poems, story and novels. It is a proud for my mother, my mother is the goddess of my poetry, she is my inspiration. Hence the book '*INDIAN HEARS*' is dedicated to my mother, Ramsakhia Devi.

Contents

Contents

Contents

Acknowledgements

If someone has well command on a language, he or she may not be an author, because only language doesn't make someone an author. The incidents and the experience of the incidents that occur in someone's life help to be an author. I am from a village that is quite in rural area, where there is no rays of English language. There people can not imagine to learn English even to read and to speak, but I imagined to be an author in English languagre. The circumstances and incidents of my life motivated me to write my emotions and thoughts. The birth of an author lies in the emotions that come from incidents and experience, and the way of decorating his or her emotions in words.

The author, Ranjan Yadav

1. Indian Hearts

Welcome to India, here all the hearts beat,
In the freezing winter, in the summer's heat,
In the peaceful dream, in the harsh-hazards,
In the sleeping sages and walking wizards.

You will find in fields, the playing children,
As diverse blossoming flowers in the garden,
In the aged people, gathered past streams,
That kick the fear, and conceive the dreams.

Our martyred forefathers, are still brave,
One feels beating their hearts, near to grave.
On the *rath* of love and peace, they did ride,
They did not provok, the path of pride or genocide.

In town, in village, in farming field or in marts,
Wherever you walk, you shall find beatig hearts.
Cottage is more lovely than the house of hatred
Happiness dies soon, that comes from fancy bed.

It's our glory, that the head of India is held high,
But not like the arrogant, in pride that die,
Ask the intellectuals of the world, they know,

At the doors of Love and Peace, India does bow.

2. The Mistake of Shakespeare

Ha! Ha! No doubt, Shakespeare,
For his achievement, is very dear,
With wit and pen, built a vast literary mart,
He decorated, he won the world's heart.

I'm not so wise, yet I went amazed,
When a line penned by him, I gazed,
"Frailty, thy name is woman."
Shakespeare! Is a woman not a part of human?

Or was Shakespeare not a procreation of,
Whom he named, the frailty stuff?
Was he unconscious, climbing on top-tower?
Was he not aware of woman's procreative power?

The time he wrote, women were literary dumb,
But by their inner sense, they did never succumb.
A woman should not have been given such name,
By which millions of son may feel shame.

Shakespeare! Here line could be used other,
It doesn't offend only Hamlet's mother---

Oh! Annoying! How in one spotted name,
Shakespeare fused all the women's fame?

3. A Sold Boy of America

I was very young, less was my age,
I wailed, I cried, but I couldn't rage...
My neighbour took me to a king,
He sold me and got a golden-ring.
I was a child, but I was sold as a sheep,
I cried a lot, urged to leave, I was hurt deep,
As I was very young, I could not do anything,
I opened my mouth wide, and began to sing:

"My mother was a black,
And that dad, a white---
I know not, what was wrong,
And what was right,
With my mother, he slept,
And before my birth, he left,
Neighours called my mom whore,
Nay! I can't sing this song anymore...
On the name of love, White father lied,
So leaving me, my black mother died."

4. Stand Nude Before Him

Stand nude before him, in the dark night,
To accomplish desires, without a fight...
Being invisible, and breaking the fence,
He comes and touches to arouse sense.

Let him pass through the back-black gate,
And when he touches, you must wait---
Remember, he is an artist, a perfect painter,
To arouse the sense, he touches the centre.

When he finds the centre, he holds it tight,
To uproot the root of sin, to fit spiritual light,
In the house of flesh, he comes with paint,
So that on the death bed, you may not repent.

5. Gonzelo

Hey Gonzelo, wait a bit,
Next to you, I shall sit;
And stroke your white hair,
And urge to make me, your pair.

> Believe in me, I won't trick,
> Ah! Your love in heart does prick,
> Restless! It doesn't let me sleep,
> In midnight, I sit and sigh deep.

I, from black, you from white,
I'm short, and long is your height,
Gongelo! I love, but I fear to get,
Will you love, to glorify my fate?

6. My Dark House

Peep into my house, it is built of dust---
The inner part is decorated with the pictures;
Of love, hatred, jealousy, greed and lust,
In the centre, two portraits of blessing and curse.

None has peeped yet, into my dark house,
But I know the convulsion of pictures in dark,
There is war and fear as of cat and mouse,
Fearful night sees, bathing in venom of a lark.

The Sun rays fall on the roof, with sharp light:
The gate of house is locked with feelings dense,
So, that rays can't peep inside as black or white,
The light of spirit breaks the gate, for entrance.

When the collapsing comes, for the house of dust,
I, the owner of this house, won't be able to rage,
In no time, all the portraits and pictures will burst:
Neighbours will go spectators, waxen wings in cage.

7. A Bed on the Head

A bed on the head, for the dead;
Woolen-soft, the colleagues made,
In the deserted land, carried for long,
And they sang sympathetic song.

''In the path of grave, none is brave,
Digger is the king, the dead is slave.''
When emotion stopped, breath did cease,
The corpse going in grave, got prestige,

When this corpse was not dead,
Grin faces of colleagues did fade...
As if he snatched wallets from them;
And when he was in pain, none came.

In the garden, all flowers blossom and fade
But go to grave in garland, when one is dead.

8. Love of a Leaf

The neighbours were green, but deaf,
It's a sad love-tale of a luckless leaf---
It too, was in the womb of mother-stem,
And then this hidden leaf had no name;
In curved shape, mother stood in mud,
Yet, this sprouted in alluring-apical bud.

The thin axil in stem connected to petiole,
Was butting its tip to soothe the soul---
Breathing and soothing, what the gender!
Venules were filaments, midrib was slender.
It had no blood-of-betrayal, running in vein,
It danced in breeze, and sipped autumn rain.

That soft breeze touched its tender part,
O Leaf! The emotion passed in the heart;
The breeze was in masque, it turned into beast,
Then strong wind shot the petiole to make feast:
Within a day or two, the green leaf went brown,
And mourned on loss of greenness, then fell down.

On the name of love, I'll show you fall of belief,
I shall show you fall of spirit in the fall of a leaf.

9. Fire Doesn't Burn

Fire!
　　Not a life,
　　　　But a fearful structure,
　　　　　　In the mind.
　　　　　　　　It doesn't burn itself,
　　　　　　　　　　It quests a cause;
　　　　　　　　As some fuels,
　　　　　　Or some woods.
　　　　When fuel burns,
　　　Flame is born
　Otherwise, no existence,
Of Fire.

10. Daddy You Died

From the womb of my mother, my life did start,
And daddy! You died soon, breaking my heart---
My brothers held my head above the falling strife,
And my dream came true, through my dear wife.

The thread of dream was short, and way was long,
Rhymeless legs tumbled with no rhythm, no song:
Then I fell in the struggling ditch, and aloud I cried,
I fluttered my hope as a wingless bird, and I tried.

After a long, legs came in rhyme, and crying got rhythm,
Observing the tempo, I started to sing with beating drum;
I'm fateful, my mom is alive, I'm doomed, daddy! You are late,
Now look at me and bless from there, daddy! Now I'm a poet.

11. A whore in That City

I walk with, but meet not, what you meet,
With the same whore, in the same street,
I see conflicts between need and desire,
One side freezing ice, the other side burning fire.

Men come with desire, her flesh, she feeds,
Locking under walls, to be nude is her needs,
Or who wants to be scratched by vulture---
Putting aside her prestige, kinship and culture.

12. The Hawk on Top

On top, a hawk was perching,
He looked hither and thither,
With his beak scratching,
Little birds' eclipsing feather.
Eyes sunken but sharp,
He moved his head clock wise,
To snatch the little birds' harp,
Here is death, a bird was to demise.

The laughing little bird,
Had no enmity with the hawk,
But it was alone, not in herd,
Picking food-corn, moving on rock.
It didn't fight with anyone,
It was unknown of its own death,
The sudden attack was to be done,
To cease the little bird's breath.

Now the hawk began to gaze,
From the ambush of leaves for his prey,
The self throbbed head, he did raise,
And brooded within, the pouncing way.
He flied high with his wings silence

To snatch the innocent bird's life,
Since the little bird was in no fence,
That could protect from killing strife.

Flied and flied, then blitzed at a sudden,
And grabbed the little bird's throat,
O the little bird! How insufferable pain!
It was like in a tiger's jaw, as a goat...
With sharp beak, he tore the throat apart,
And sucked the blood, there was no flood,
Here stopped, the little bird's beating heart,
The hawk flied, hoping to grab another bird.

13. Pleasure of Love

Shut up! Thou have pride beyond---
Of thy sprouting flesh;
And tease me keeping at distance.
Who will ask for love in old age?
When this fair flesh hangs in bones,
Fair blonde! Assist in love, do not rage.

Myth of spiritual love, kills pleasure,
Pleasure of love is in the love of flesh,
Platonic love is, but a path of purgation,

And spiritual love, like a meditation.
Hence I beseech, to decrease the distance,
Delay will witness, the decaying of beauty:
Time is less, let's ride on the vehicle of flesh,
To reach in the palace of pleasure.

14. A Man of No Crime

A fugitive was spotted in the street,
Looking around, fleeing on bleeding feet,
And the crowd was chasing as a leopard,
Hungry for weeks, looking a prey in the yard.

Street thorns pricked in sole, he fell down,
And the throng tore, the fugitive's gown,
An unconscious force was riding the crowd,
'Hold and beat, hold and beat', cried aloud.

No grace! He was the victim of no crime,
Fate had pushed him into the worst time:
His new beloved had deceived him in faith,
A lone son from former wife, met to death.

The debt was huge, taken from neighbour,
Fortune had fallen, nothing was in his favour,
The crowd became cats, he, a scared mouse,
So he tried to run away, leaving his house.

Mad! The hunger of crowd was filled,
Sad! A man of no crime, was killed.

15. The Way of Worship

Is thy worship granted in Almighty's feet,
And mine is denied by Him to meet?
Thou worship to get thy goal,
And I, for the peace of my soul,
Thou go to the place of worship,
Light the incense sticks, and try to be His kinship,
Not to heal thy sinful wound and shun thy lust,
Thou go to worship to add more dust in thy dust.

The place of worship does not exist,
At day, at night, in shadow or in mist,
It's a state of soul, for perfection and peace:
When we worship within, worship is this.
If hatred holds thy heart and jealousy does prevail,
Thy door of heaven is locked, thou meet the hell.
If, for the sake of ruling the weak, you fight,
Thou aren't His kinship, thou get no virtuous light.

The lightening of incense sticks, brings no such fragrance,
That can cherish the wounded soul and absorb the tense,
No bit of offering sweets, the Almighty does eat,
When thy soul is honest and pure, to Him thou meet.

16. The Red Rose

The wave of the sea water comes and goes,
This is not with the beauty of red rose---
Once comes in petal and blossoms with hues,
And in the morning, we find on, pearl like dews:
With fragrance far, in the garden, outside the garden;
Then bees and flies suck the beauty, leaving in pain.

Bees and flies suck, preparing their invisible bed,
And the Red Rose loses all its hues and does fade,
O the Red Rose! You come, blossom, and get pain...
Once you lose your fragrance, it won't come again.

17. Wingless Falcon

The gang of temptress plays the guitar of greed,
And the wingless falcons fall in enticing tone,
The soul tries to retreat, but lust does lead,
The mind provokes lust, and the soul feels alone.

Alluring rhythm draws falcons more near,
And the temptress presents forked-feast,
Whispering, 'eat my feast without any fear'...
While eating, drag your beak deep, being a beast.

18. An Aadiwasi Mother

When a queen is pregnant,
She sits on the soft-sofa,
And walks on the velvet red:
And sleeps in the queen's bed.
She is cared like a worthy treasure,
And the palace plays in pleasure.

I'm a son of an Aadiwasi mother,
When I was in her womb,
She went to work in other's field,
She went to the forest,
To bring the bundle of dry wood logs,
To cook food, burning in soil-hearth,
She brought water in soil-pot
From a well, dug far away,
She wore old tattered clothes,
And sat, on the cot of broken legs.

No knight, and no palace, she had---
She gave me birth in the house,
Where bushes were the walls,
And palm leaves were the thatch,
From far, neighbours could peep,

For it was not a house but a cottage.

When a queen gives birth to a child,
Many doctors and nurses are there;
And the yard of the king seems a fair.
My mother was returning from waging-field,
And I was born in the mid-way---
There was no doctor, and no nurse,
The bed of my birth was earth.
My mother was hungry and feeling pain:
So she ate some wild-fruits,
When she got hiccup, drank the water of rain.

19. Moon Come Soon

Moon, Moon, come soon near,
Hold my hand, remove my fear,
Mom is sleeping, night is   dark,
Out of the door, many dogs bark.

Moon, Moon, come soon near,
Hold my hand, remove my fear;
My doll is lost in dark, father is far,
And roof stops, the twinkling star.

Filled with fear, I'm poor, you are rich,
In the corner, seems ghost and witch
Moon, Moon, come soon near,
Hold my hand, remove my fear.

20. A Sage in My Dream

Like a child, I was walking with a gentle sage,
Quite old with long white beard, yet he did rage,
Of his fleeing age and walked, with step long,
Guiding me the path of life, with singing song;
The song of spirituality, he sang in ecstasy,
And told, the worth of life in perfection, not in fantasy.

Holding my hand, he taught two ways of life,
One leading to perfection, other to strife,
"My son, the way of perfection is difficult to go,
And the path deviators would never show,
You the right path, on each step it will tease,
And the path of strife will draw inwards at ease."

Then I promised the sage, to walk on the right way,
Refraining from deviators, I'll touch the spiritual ray,
How thorny my path be, I'll walk picking the thorn,
O my dear sage! Since, again I would not be born,
I would give up ill paths, and walk on the right one,
When I succeed, you would bless, saying well done.

21. Touch My Waist

Touch my waist, you will feel,
Inside bubbling breath, outer still,
My legs are grabbed under the clay
Height of breast is high, looks in May,
And you don't have feathers to fly,
Nor your hands are so long to try,
You do not, but I read your tongue,
If I'm healthy, healthy is your lung.

Many one come and put their legs on my head,
As I'm their bride, I'm their resting bed---
Sometime, alone, sometime come in pair,
And have oozing romance, scattering hair.
O dear human! Don't think like animal herds,
I am an old tree, and they are beloved birds.

22. The World of Betrayal

The sun will not fall, on the bed of the Moon,
The bottom of sea won't come on the surface,
But a king will lose his heart, in a lady-love,
And the queen will play the game of betrayal.
A kingdom comes in hand, through the card,
Honesty is trampled, and hoaxers get reward.
I'll show you America in India, through the map,
No upheaval, no threatening, it's quite peaceful.

Human world is the world of flattery and fantasy,
Here the throne is held by the hands of hypocrisy,
Be aware, be in stream, while chasing the dream,
Or path deviators pull behind to make you scream.
Be aware, here truth is crushed by the bulk of lie
The beings of wings creep, and wingless beings fly.

23. Leopard Life

Circumstances pull my force behind,
Pain pricks in heart, and restless is mind.
In empty wallet, a huge debt, I'll have to toil hard,
I'll have to fly like a kite, and run like a leopard.

I want to hasten my way, but sliding pulls back,
What if engine hurls, and wheels are not on track.
Wrong paths hurt me, hence I choose the right,
I'm burning fuel, but I have no lamp, so, no light.

I shall always toil hard, how strenuous life is,
I'll keep fluttering till my breath does cease.
As I bear a huge debt, I shall have to toil hard,
I'll have to fly like a kite, and run like a leopard.

24. This is My Country

This is my country,
And these are citizens---
In map, the land is vast,
In census, huge population,
The map has been divided,
Into thousand of parts,
And people of the land;
Walk with their broken hearts.

Oh! The sound of beating drum---
Thy rhythm soothes the ears,
And seems pleasurable from far,
But when the listeners come near,
They see wound of thy scratched heart...
And thy soul, butting to beaters.

25. Myna Dancing in Winter

I was passing through the way, one morning,
I was riding on my bike, and bitterly shivering,
Heavy winter, ops! It was extremely cold;
It wouldn't spare anyone, if young or old.

But what I saw, was wonder, quite amazing,
Mynas were chirping, dusting and dancing,
Some in the bushes, some sliding on the rocks,
In such winter, quite naked, no gloves, no shocks.

I gazed and pondered staying there, for a while,
My teeth were cluttering, and they had smile---
No sweater, no shelter, all the seasons are same,
O lovely birds! You are made of what frame!

26. Dhyan Chand: The Great

The world came, and tried to shrink the fate,
But this promising land has always been great;
Our culture was damaged, minds made slave,
Intricate, yet sons of the land were coming brave.

Your contribution, submission and patriotism,
Have made a huge tower, the tower of strugglism,
The magic of Hockey, from you, the world learnt,
But in own land, now that stick seems weak and burnt.

When the invaders made this esteemed land a mart,
In Hockey, You were showing your magic and art;
From the pious womb of mother India, a son bold,
You struggled a lot, and three times, you won gold.

For the world, you are a champion son of a champion land,
When the hope of victory is broken, your magic can mend;
It can fill with hope and inspiration the valiant who feel sick,
O the warrior of Hockey! The world went amazed at your
stick.

Now this land seems running behind some invisible treasure,

That may be the treasure of wealth or of momentary pleasure,
People are rattling and, in trouble to have a big house in town,
And in this vast land, Literature, sports, and arts are going
down.

27. The Beating Drum

A drum makes no sound itself,
The sound comes after beating,
A thick stick beats in the heart,
And the variation of beating,
Engenders the rhythm and tones.

Listeners are happy with good tones,
Who looks at the scratches in dermis?
Ethnicity feels the wound of the drum.
O the bloodless drum! You can't bleed,
By eyes blind, where the tears fall from?

How the being of blood avail pleasure from pain,
When this tongueless drum is beaten as a toy,
Quite in toxic mood, the being of blood enjoy,
The beater knows the wound, and the pain,
But helpless, helpless, can't stop from beating.

28. The Hidden Beast

I'm weak and sick, and deprived of ability,
Yet let me bear, the bags of responsibility,
The responsibility of beating the beast;
That killed my dad and snatched my feast.

My mother is alive, her hair has turned white,
The ears hear no sound, eyes have no sight---
Nor does she know the reason of demise of dad,
Happiness is eclipsed, so she wails and be sad.

As I'm weak and sick, O dead dad bless me to heal,
That unkind brut beast, one day surely I will kill,
Like Shakespeare's Hamlet, I would not pretend,
Of being mad and wait for detecting thy death land.

Believe, on my tongue-tip, I would find the fact,
And the cause you were crushed, I shall detect;
For the sake of revenge, I won't kill the beast,
But the brut-beast may not snatch more feast.

29. Hatred

Where from comes this hatred?
And in my heart, who does place its bed?
I can't look that, where does it lie,
But I'm sure, it too will die, when I die.

When does it germinate, and reap?
Is this harmful-hatred Love's kinship?
Why in the same house it does live?
Love conceives goodness, Hatred does deceive.

At the entrance of Hatred, Negativity fills in mind,
And lovely people with good heart, go quite blind.

30. The Poor Students

Everyone has, the will of Education,
But fails to face, the severe situation,
Though, tries to be brave and bold,
Alas! Life is gripped in distinct fold.

Having no horse for race, on foot is ride,
They come from villages, some town's side,
Sometime no money to pay, so they weep,
Sometime no food to eat, so, hungry they sleep.

Today's Education is sold, at heavy rate,
Is this precious gem not in their fate?
They toil a lot, but get nothing else tears,
Tense of losing chance, frustration and fears.

The poor students hope from the men of coats,
But men of coats are busy in sailing own boats,
None does care the promising pearls of poor men,
As their fates are banned, and born to bear pain.

What would they feel, while writing in a slate?
What would they feel, when passing in graduate?
Oh! worry not, He is helper, and He does help,

Schooling a lesson, keep toiling, have faith in self.

31. Love in Winter

Eyes flashed like corals, and lips as lute,
With teeth within, as white strings:
And in the centre of countenance,
A bit of molesting-mole, as a coral in a crown.
The beauty of the beloved obliterated,
The flaming Sun, and the redness of Mars.
She was like Helen, but elevated in height,
Lookers walked in haste, in infatuated light.

The running blood of vein, dropped in a tub,
And infatuation was born in the masque of love,
The beloved had been wooed for one day,
So the lover was brooding over the loving-way,
Ah! A bucket of love, under the blanket,
The lover bestowed in winter, to his beloved.

32. On the Road

No road to take to the road,

Where I used to get vehicles

To go to my destination of learning,

I came out from my home on foot,

I walked miles, putting a sack of rice,

Sometime of potatoes and wheat

On my shoulder as a poor coolie.

Once while going, my leg slipped in a ditch,

I fell in the ditch and broke my one leg.

When I reached to the road, uff, no vehicle...

I waited for hours, sitting on the Earth,

Losing my all enthusiasm, hope and mirth;

After long, some motor vehicles came,

I raised my hand to stop, and urged to take me in,

But most of the vehicles were full of passengers.

Waiting and waiting, how long one can wait,

I used to get tired, irritated and hopeless,

Then after hours, some vacant vehicle came,

And I used to get in, to reach my destination.

I can never forget those haunted days.

33. A Doomed Lady

I'm a lone lady, all come to vex,
The regime knocks the door for tax,
And playboys knock the door for sex.
What can I do, if I am fair and young,
If looking at me your hearts are hung,
Do not lengthen your watering tongue.
Infusion, not at hand, but I can read,
And foretell the trail, they use to lead,
But can't say, they are of what seed---

With these hands, I buried my lone son,
In nation's war, my lover's life has gone,
Yet around my mansion, libertines run.
They glimpse from far, my flesh is fair,
And come near with intent, to scare,
O the morons, let me live, spare, spare.
If hearts are wild, if you can not feel,
Come to me and being brute-beasts, kill,
Then your wild-wounded hearts may heal...

34. Happy Birthday to a Muslim Friend

Why should I wish on your birthday?
Your religion doesn't come in my way,
You'r from Mosque, I am from Temple,
We hold different names, what does resemble?
Oh! My soul says something, if we are bound,
Let me harken and meditate over the sound...
Nay! I should wish, on my friend's birthday,
We divide ourselves, we come through one way.

Hey! I try to get, God of ours, Allah of yours,
Are the same, powerful and invisible force,
Ya, my dear, They are one, and we too are one,
I will wish you, in ecstasy, and with renown.
If I am a flower, you must be of it's fragrance,
Let's rest in the lap of humanity, burying tense.

35. My Shoes

Sparrows do not play the lutes of lust,
They pick grains, perching on the dust.
In gluttonous house, of ravening hawk,
Sparrows get death, without any shock.
Scuffling sparrows pick grain after grain,
To make prey, ravening birds go insane;
Toilers are in mass, penetrators are less,
Sparrows try to hide, but interlopers trace.

They said to me, these are my black shoes,
But when I put my feet in, shoes came lose,
Treachery crushed my credence and emotion,
Yet I bore the lose shoes, it was my devotion.
Tyrants strike hard, on the bones of the weak,
And leave at the door of death, making them sick.

36. My Village: Asnatari

Commoners bow their heads, before the crown,
Greenness lies in village, town goes with brown.
Welcome to arena of Asnatari, It is a small village,
Pollution-hills are not here, but nature's salvage.
Situated in nature's lap, what a beautiful shape!
If you meet to aroma, your sense will never escape,
River Badua hugs my village, in two sides it flows,
Weavers cross the river, when soothing breeze blows:

In the rest two sides, you'll meet a standing mountain,
Full of trees and herbals, the visitors wish to visit again,
On the mountain head, birds meet wandering waves,
And in the lap, some animals rest in little caves.
From the dents of rocks, from feet, water leaks,
The gurgling of water seems, as something it speaks.
Far from the chaotic-crowd, it has tranquil atmosphere,
Breath out of stink, we inhale, things and beings all are sheer.

Most of the dwellers, dwell in the house of mud,
On the thatch, young bee comes to love young bud,
Children play in dust, they have shepherers charm,
Old people are engaged in caws, goats and few farm.
Quarrelling of mother-in-law and daughter-in-law,

Shows the old custom of village with little flaw.
There is also a bit trail of jealousy in neighbour,
Someone stands in against, someone in favour.

In the world of tacky-technology and menacing-modernity,
You can find here antique gems of fidelity and fraternity,
The aged-adventures with hanging skins work all the days,
In farming-fields, in scorching sun, like black wood, they blaze,
When the Earth rotates apposit the Sun, and path loses in dark,
For their home, the shephered-like adventures in haste embark;
When they reach home, their eyes quest their grand-offsprings
To tell the story of ghosts, witches, fairies, queens and of kings.

No crowd of madness, nature sprinkles harmony and balm,
To air away the ador of disaster, to keep my village calm...
Others may say it full of fallacy, but I assume as good fate,
It is worthy beyond, taking birth in such a peaceful hamlet.

37. The Barbarians

The barbarians, bathe in blood,
And consume the flesh of commoners,
Sowing the seeds of horror,
Are the barbarians unrivalled?
Sitting in the virge of death,
Make the innocence sing funeral dirge,
For the coronation of self crown,
Darkening commoners' new dawn,
Blistering with disgusted wit,
The barbarians leave the skeletons.

O the commoners, arouse your strength,
Let your frozen fear melt in the rays of liberty,
If you want to vision of new dawn,
The redness of the Sun with own eyes...
Then let your hands hold spades,
And hit the barren land to dig graves,
And let the brutes be buried alive...
Your visions have been lost...
But the new commers would look,
New dawn, with their own eyes.

38. Interaction

When we interact with someone or something
The flashing of some images exist there,
Through the beauty, badness, words or gesture
Of the people and things we come across,
That images are saved in the box of our experience,
And when we again meet and talk to some others,
We open the box of that experience,
And select the effective words to effect the people.

Experience does not come from the single one,
We meet, we talk and we observe...
Rather it is a cocktail of interactions,
Of meeting and facing uncounted people and incidents,
From books, from the moment of pleasure and pain,
From the seasons like summer, winter and rain.

39. Playing Guitar

In drought, I was playing on a guitar,
She heard the swooning music,
Stayed for a while, and hastened towards me,
Gasping, she came, but stood a bit far.

The rise and fall of tones,
Conceived an enticing rhythm,
And she matched her feet with the tempo,
Unaware of her presence, near me,
I beautified more the rhythm,
I aired the tempo, and kept on playing.

Listening the music of guitar,
Coming and standing a bit far,
She danced, and danced, and danced,
For hours, unaware of her feet-pain.

Some thorns pricked in sole,
And the soil under her sole,
Got shower from her blood,
Yet, constantly she danced.
If the music is injected in vein,
Death at stake, gives no pain.

Suddenly I stopped playing,
Soon she stopped too, and cried,
Staring at me in fainting voice
And came more near to me...

And she whispered in swooning voice-
''Music is the herbs to heal the wound,
Love! Play on! Play on! It soothes the soul.''
I was stuck at, then started playing again,
She laughed aloud, as a witch of faerie,
Then she vanished, and thunder brought rain.

40. A Refugee Father

Gazing his sick child, lying on a mat,
What father! What father would do that?
One could see the bones, in stomach, no meal,
Weakness was engulfing, no medicine to heal.

Doomed father uprooted, some grass root,
And shook the lying child's hand and foot,
Father! Oh! The kind father did weep,
And the soar tears, by his lips he did sip.

At night, this father met horrible sight,
From back to next, from left and right,
Everywhere, hungry children were crying,
As breathing fish, at the time of frying.

Many neighbour children lost their breath,
And his own child too, was to meet to death:
Oh! Father kept crying, calling the child's name
But to save this doomed child no saviour came.

Suddenly stopped, all the hopeful tones,
The lying child went cold, it had no response,
Father understood, now the child was no more,

He wailed in words, "What should he live for?"

Already, all the hair from head had fallen down,
And on the body, this child had no gown…
The doomed father oiled the child's bald head,
And prepared himself, his own child's death bed.

Like a fearful ghost, this father was spared,
Oh! The child died, whom as a soul, he cared.

41. The Three Words

On the passionate pyre, I was burnt,
And falling on fire, I have learnt...
In my rest life, I shall say to none,
''I Love You'', even burning as the Sun.
I will love someone, more than her,
But the three words will never occur,
I shall make her feel love in each vein,
In excited mirth, and in pricking pain.

I shall make her feel love, in each hair-hole,
I shall make her feel love, in sublimed soul,
I would prefer to be kicked in horrible-hell
But those disgusting words, I'll never tell.
Thousand times, with my meek-mouth I told,
''I Love You, '' and I tried, her hand, to hold,
I loved her from my heart, deep and deep,
I voiced, but she never heard, so I did weep.

I know not, who will love her more than me,
But, If I die before her, the almighty will see.

42. Leaving the City

Let me go far, from this crowded town,
Ill-will is spreading, goodness going down,
Neighbours walk on the path that is jealous,
My flesh is well, but the heart can't bear thus.

We get the Plant, we sow in the Earth,
But people do not be the same, as at birth.
I see going down, the crops of humanism,
And flourishing the crops of egocentrism.

Here nothing is spiritual, here nothing is moral,
People use people, not as people but as a coral,
Friendship reflects on the high wall of wealth,
None to ask, in empty wallet and poor health.

Love lies in fair flesh, and in sprouted parts,
Science has crushed the beauty of Arts,
Talk through technology is emotionless,
Even kinships talk less, face by face.

All are engulfed in self, no pain, no pity,
So I am going far, from this crowded city.

43. A Poor Farmer

Miles away, from his cottage
Dusty beard, scattered as hedge,
On the chest, a hanging shield,
Tattered clothes, sitting in field,
A small piece, the farmer is sad,
Stood up holding in hand a spade;
No ox, no coulter, yet started to toil,
By hands, digging the drought soil..

Loyal, and passionately, soil he dug,
As a beloved to her lover, does hug,
Happy as a child at king's palace is born,
Sprinkled water and sowed some corn.
Germinated, grew up, ready for feast,
Oh! The destroyer came as a wild beast.

44. Death Before Birth

A baby was killed in the womb,

And it was buried in the tomb,

As a child it could not be born,

So from its tomb, it does mourn,

"Mom, my mom, before my birth,

Why I was buried under the Earth...

Was I an unwanted wave from the sea?

Love between you resulted into me,

You were of today, I was of tomorrow,

I gave you what the pain, what the sorrow?

I was playing in your pious womb,

Mom, my mom, now I'm in a tomb,

Insects are eating flesh, I cry in pain

Can such sin be washed by holy rain?

I weep, how this world is mean,

What sin can be bigger than this sin.

I too wanted to see the world's sight,

Nature, Love, hatred, pleasure or plight,

But I was strangled brutally in womb,

And sent as Satan in a dark tomb.

Dad, my dad, I cry in the grave, do you hear?

Mom, my mom, sin was done, do you fear?

45. Fear

Fear, fear, flag of fear, who hosts?
Look here children fear of ghosts…
As fleeing away rats,
From the mouth of cats.
In throne, the fear of kings lies,
With coming down crown dies.
Lovers hide their fear in rose,
Thieves fear of being expose.
Fear of sinners weakens their hearts,
And artists fear of their vulgar arts.

46. Destruction by Fire

The destruction came, wrapped in fire flame,
People looked, people laughed, shame, shame,
Horrible fire! The fire was not blowing off...
Scarcity of water, finding a way was tough.

Heartless neighbours as wind strong,
Fueled the fire, with destructive song,
It became a burning Ghat, within an hour,
Here burning of my hope, falling of tower.

I dropped water, by my drinking pots,
One pot, two pots, then water came shorts.
I looked the destruction, with my sad mood,
Then laughing as a lunatic, at distance I stood.

47. Divine Effort

Within your branch, keep your thorn,
Since, with my own pain, I am born.
Passing through the crowd of flesh,
Breath continues in critical race...
Yet efforts do not stop to shine,
Through the deeds, through divine.
No hope of help, the journey is long,
One lives and dies, singing self-song.

48. The Death of Beauty

A beautiful flower was in the garden,
Sprouted from a little bud of hues,
Under the garden inviting aroma,
And the fragrance was outside too.
A wanderer came from above the fence,
He lulled the flower with his lute,
And tried to woo, to grant his love...
Bows down to innocence, it was granted.

Then the wanderer came more near,
And tried to taste morning dropped dews,
Dropped on the flesh of the flower,
Inhaling the fragrance, unveiling the hues.
The flower believed in him, in breeze it slept,
When it awoke, with no beauty it was left.

49. My Leda

Why my soul does hire,
That thrills my substances
Into the flame of burning fire?
Surely, this heart was hard,
But the love of my Leda turned it,
Into a shaking-swamp;
Now no colleague or science,
Seems to dry up the swamp.

Neither any natural heat is fit.
Waves of sea fear to come near,
To cool the invisible passion-provoked heat.
As love soothes love, one can resolve,
Being an abstract, charismatic,
That is love-logy of my lovely Leda.

50. An Unemployed Youth

As a wingless bird, I flutter and wander,
In streets, on roads, in quest of work...
I walk, from the bottom of my gender,
Like an ill, nomadic and refugee Turk.

I was happy playing in dust, in childhood,
Now I'm young, playing in dust has gone,
Hunger in stomach knows none, but food,
And hanged responsibilities on backbone.

I'm not a politician, nor I'm a preaching-sage,
None to help in earning, no wealth to invest,
In vast land, I'm a parrot and I live in a cage,
Who crushes my vision, I assume him a guest.

I perceive, I ponder, ways of the world's act,
A little pebble lied on path, seems a big hill,
I work a lot, but no soothing breath in fact,
I feel as broken bud from branch of my will.

As a fearful-frog, I go in poisonous snakes' yards,
In quest of work, I stand in fear at death-door,

There are many hidden snakes as brute-wards,
Snakes raise head to bite, I flee to my own shore.

So many times, I tried to build my own fort,
But the paths were full of thorns, and dense,
To justify my struggle here, there is no court,
Now I live at a place where is no fort, no fence.

51. O The Slumber

O the Slumber, why do you not come to me?
Forgot the way? Or drowned in some sea?
I lay on the bed, and turn my body side by side,
Anxiety of life keeps coming as wave and tide.

O the Slumber, my slumber, at least come and sit,
In my bed and look my convulsion, if not fit,
In my eyes, and console my panic heart,
Why my life has become a sleepless mart.

I try to sleep but this empty life lets me not sleep,
Thoughts come in bulk and goes in heart deep,
And break the slight-slumber, keep awoken,
Leaving my bed, I walk in yard, kitchen and lane.

And again I go in bed, try to sleep closing my eyes
Yet this sweet-slumber does not come, where it dies?
O the Slumber, my Slumber, come and make me sleep,
Or I shall die as a waterless fish, as in fisher's ship.

52. Desire

No life is giant as the universe,
Meteorites fall yet, on the terse,
The rotation has lost the speed,
And revolution, the head to lead.

No shelter, for this wandering dust,
It begins the revolution as army-gust,
On the orbits of acquiring dusty desire,
And it ends in grave, and some in fire.

53. What is True Love

If you come in birth, all will vex,
Here people live for food and sex.
Love seems lie, where does it lie,
When in unusual war, soldiers die.
Love has no bounds, and no fates,
But here people have two wallets,
One filled with love, in other hatred lies,
If it lives for the first, and for the last it dies...
Ha ha ha, Love! It's not love but need,
To quench the hunger, that does feed.

54. The Green Woods

Here comes the green wood, on its feet,
Avoid the falling thorns from the passing way,
It would walk the whole night, and the whole day,
And the hopeless beings, parched in the sun, will meet.

This green wood walks waving the banks in its own mood,
It is reluctant of being stopped by its kinship or stranger,
It wants to dance in its own step, as a liberty-loving passenger,
Rebukes all the weathers bad in way, and takes digestive food.

Who can catch the tail of a leopard, when running in race,
On the mid path, cattle of small legs and less flash rattle,
And are wounded by each other, this green wood ends their battle,
Applying the healing herbs brought by breeze, to make pain less.

Though the clouds are going, the sky will not fall on the head,
Monsoon would come with nepenthes, rain to water singed crops,
Be hopeful beings, do not weep, wipe the eyes, the falling drops,

Flowers of fragrance with dappled hues, will fall on bride's bed.

55. Long is the Way

From the womb of mother, the way starts,
And till the labour pain, in dark, talk the two hearts,
Moves on a little circle till the stepping on the Earth,
And the way is lengthened more with the birth;
Little-life, sliding on the sleeping set, side by side,
Has less to interact but caring by mother as a guide,
And sucking its own fingers, assuming as milk feeding,
Plays the little-life in pleasure, till its innocence is leading.

Hairless grey head, and in unreadable words it cries,
What the infant wants to tell, to get its mother tries,
The way is lost in dark, and eyes are not ready to find,
Eyes look the sight, eyes are not blind, but less is the mind.
Till it walks on its little foot with whistling boot,
The way seems easy, but in fact life has long route.

56. Hopeless Life

Let me hold the broken-branch of my life,
What would I do, else being a visitor...
I visit the vast fountains of grief,
And hear in harness, the voice of cry.

In my happy days, I thought to wear wings,
For flying, and to perch on my decorated-dream,
As parent birds make nest with tiny grasses,
To keep their eggs-and-young safe from hazards.

Now I look my life as a forest of no green trees,
And running breath, as dispersed dust in desert,
Where no oxygen to breathe, no water to drink,
My dust might be distorted in time unaware.

Yet some breathing-dusts hope much,
From my hopeless decaying dust...
Hoping is no crime, it is innocence,
And unknown of the grief, I'm passing through.

Stopping the way to grave is inevitable,
But my feet seem stepping much faster...
My wish is to leave some sign behind,

But tattered-time push from back to grave.

57. The Rape of the Heart

Horrible! Horrible! Horses are flying,
And all the flying birds are creeping,
Humans are turning into animal-shape,
Come in light to look the Heart's rape.
Plants are growing vast without seeds,
Passion is dying being trapped in weeds,
Walk the world, and watch the each life,
For each life you'll find a house of strife.

Tony loved a princess, comely and fair,
He assured her to marry, to make his pair,
The princess too loved him as a mother to son:
When he played with her flesh, she thought it fun,
Oh! Tony left the princess using as a thing of mart,
And in the shadows of love, he raped her heart.

58. Human and the Rose

The wisest may hardly be as happy as roses,
Roses blossom, laugh and move within the circle,
They do not look at, what calamities befall on...
Instead, blossom avoiding the thorns aside,
And spread their fragrance miles away,
To make the saddened happy, teaching a lesson.

We the wisest of the unfathomed world,
Break the boundaries of the circle we live in,
And burn within in invisible fire for damn sense,
We wash out the mind of nature's existing law,
And swiftly make unjustified, hazardous law,
That is dark to eye at, and hard to chew and digest.

Wanton is to make a fort, full of trivial treasures,
In that fort, can we meet the roses' pleasures?
How human can sit and fit on the rose-branch,
The fountains of true happiness lie on the faces,
That have no sharp weapons to harm others,
Here Nature is the super mother of all mothers.

59. True Love is Not Honoured

For your wanton-wish, you loved me half,
For love's sake, I loved you deep, and deep,
So chuckling cheeks, parting lips you laugh,
And holding heart, pressing my pain, I weep.
I kept my faith in your swamp-shaking faith,
Trapped me in mire, and left a thing of nothing,
Intention was to suffocate my running-breath,
Altering the sun of my life, forever into evening.

Breathing is a halt, where fragile flesh does stay,
For sometimes as the shadows of something in sun,
The darkness of night begins with the passing of day,
We too would pass away, here is nectar to none,
Medium of love is flesh, yet people make heart hard,
Here true loving hearts are torn, and get panic reward.

60. I Put a Picture

What I eat, I digest,
I digest too, what I eat not---
You know not, the mental food,
See people chewing hard wood,
To quench the troubled mood.

I do, you too, and all do,
Eat the mental-meat---
Look at the Lizard on the wall,
By a snake it was spared,
But the little locusts are scared.

Scared, for the Lizard would hunt,
And the Lizard has to digest,
The tiniest meat, it eats...
As well as the food-of-fear,
That, that the snake could tear.

I'm not a painter, yet I put a picture,
Come, see and be aware, today you eat,
You too will be eaten tomorrow...
And you not, but the new comers will know,
Whoever eats, becomes the things of eating.

61. A Tree of Love

A tree of love, I planted,
And watered it incessantly,
Being a savior, I saved it
From venomous airy worms,
From celestial thunderstorms.
I bestowed soothing aura,
But, I sowed no seeds of desire.
The tree of love grew in full-green
And the beating boughs planted will,
The will of shadows and fruits,
The tossing leaves in breeze planted
The will of breathing...
And the buds panted,
The pre-dream of flowers,
And then the flowers gave birth,
To the hopes of fruits.
Then I learnt---
In this sinful earth,
Desires take birth.

62. An Elegy on the Village

Now, nothing has that taste,

For my lung, or tongue,

I had heard the melody,

The singing melody of birds,

In the time of dawn and dusk,

And with proud, hearts were swollen.

I had tasted the farms in soil brown,

Plough on shoulder, stick in hand,

Men going with their oxen---

Then their ladies later on foot,

Going to the ploughing field, taking foods.

I had met many ones--

The aged ones with folks and tales,

With their grand children,

Happy men, with no wealth in wallet.

Now, the village has become a town,

In every evening, the gathering of family

Has fallen apart into modernity,

Children are lost in the tales of technologies,

And the grandparents feel...

The pain of alienation and lonesome,

Now the oxen of the peasants have gone---
The singing melody of the birds has gone---
And the sour taste of tongue is growing,
Now, the beauty of the village has gone...

63. My Psychology

When my psyche finds fault, it revives,
By nature, again in the same ditch dives.
Sometimes the fairy soul derives the mind,
Sometimes the very mind becomes blind.
Since long, old nerves try to find the fact,
Why with different persona, different act?
With elite ones air passes through deep lung,
With downtrodden, easily moves the tongue.

64. A Virgin Rose

In the heavy storm, in the heavy rain,
A new gardener came in the garden,
He looked all the flowers tossing heads,
As brides and grooms in the loving beds.
When the strong storm turned into breeze,
A blossoming rose, flirting with a fly at ease,
The gardener saw, the fly came and went,
Sitting on the leaf, sucking and feeling the scent.

If the drops of rain, fall on the fading crop,
Who the doomed would like this to stop---
The rose falls in the friendship with the fly,
And the gardener looked the fly as a sweet-sly,
This passionate rose, now feared to depart,
For the fly had built a house in the rose's heart.

One day the rose scattered its hue and called the fly,
The fly came, and sucked, in pain the rose did cry,
And then from the ambush, the gardener came out,
'Help! Help! Save me, save me!' The fly did shout...
Then the rose noticed, oh! The fly was no more,
Flowers of the garden began to say the rose a whore.
Said the gardener, "How long in friendship have been,

No matter, confess if you are a virgin, it is no sin.'‘

Oh! From its branch the rose fell down,

As the falling of a defeated king's crown,

And cried unveiling its scratched skin,

’’After bathing in the tub of love who is virgin.

Harken! Harken! If making love is sin,

Go in quest, none in the world is virgin.''

65. A Road Where is No Chaos

Bathing in blood, bathing in blood for years,
Wiping with the coffin, the coffin of fears:
Come, see, Death in life, and life in death,
All are breathing, but hanged in half breath.
A man can lie, but my pen is not lying,
Here people are neither living, nor dying.

Air of the lungs stops in suffocating throat,
As fixed, in the frame of sacrificing goat.
The sea of tears dried, no place of pathos
So, going in a road where there is no chaos.

66. A Doomed Child

Little, little is my foot,
Day seems dense and dark,
And long is the rout,
Far is the house, who will hark?
If I scream in fears,
I see none to wipe my tears.

My father is sick, and lies on the bed,
I'm father's rose,
Mother! Because, my mother is dead;
I take *joothan bread* in my doze...
For me, happiness is dried wood,
Yet with my sick father, I live in happy mood.

None in the way asks my name,
For, a doomed child, I am;
A rural child, I have seen no town,
Sometime naked, sometime tattered gown
I wear, all are eager to know my gender,
I am a doomed child, and my heart is tender.

67. The King is No More

Civilians are meeting, the falling fate,
The king has lost his estate;
The sun too, has not come with ray,
Glory of the estate is fading away.

In favour, civilian are mad,
And brooding over, what was bad!
Innately pearl, and on top like alpine,
The kingdom of the king did shine,

Now that glory, that has gone...
Can be, perhaps, retrieved by none;
In the sky, the shining of star,
People would see, but the king has gone far.

Civilians will meet the weeping shore,
O the dear king! Now, you are no more!

68. The Fainted Flower

Breaking all the thorny fence,
Blossomed, and the fragrance,
Spreading vastly on the tower,
Now, it is a fainted flower.

From the bottom of west and east,
Sterile starvation, feeding feast...
From the numb-north to south,
Dropped water in the thirsty mouth;

Alas! Negligence of own bread,
Earned bread for live and dead,
Died, the flower! He did fade,
And yet, the story went unsaid.

The flower went into the deep dale,
But still people can feel, when inhale,
For life, the green leafy branch may lie,
But the true fragrance does never die.

69. Death in Summer

Oh! Extreme Summer is on the head,
And human beings are dying in the bed.
With gasping, some birds are flying,
And on stubble trees, some are dying.

Nowhere is relief, nowhere is rest,
See, animals are dying in the forest.
The Earth feels thirsty, in heat wave,
Tigers too, are dying in the deep cave.

Cutting of trees, gives pain to the Earth,
Planting trees saves life and brings mirth,
We can heal and absorb the summer pain,
Planting and saving, makes the earth heaven.

70. When Fortune Falls

Thousands of streets, and paths to go,
Thousands of gods and deities to bow,
But how to know, and how to mark?
The paths are full of thorns and dark.
Standing on the thorns, bare foot, I cry,
To reverse the paths in harmony, I try,
But it is not easy for me, to retreat...
The   feet, when destiny does meet.

Consistently, with my inner force, I fight,
But alas! I see, there is no glint of light;
I repent over the mistakes, I have done,
Yet it seems, my good days have gone...
What? If you are wise, and you are brave,
When your fortune falls, none can save.

71. The Spider and Filament

At the thinnest filaments, as I looked,
My sparkling sharp sight was hooked,
A tiny spider released filaments, so long,
Like a lone-labourer, not in any throng;
Filaments after filament, it had drawn,
For it's womb-babies to make a crown.
It had no veil on the head as a poor bride,
A princess dies of hunger, sitting in pride.

This spider had been conceived, to be a mother,
So it intertwined the filaments into one another;
From one corner to the other, and in order,
Through filaments, it made soft bed and border,
And then this tiny life was going to give birth...
Bravo! What an ingenuity! On this very Earth.

www.ingramcontent.com/pod-product-compliance
Lightning Source LLC
Chambersburg PA
CBHW040823120726
48005CB00012B/1488